BIRDS
OF
NEW ENGLAND

PHOTOGRAPHY BY JIM ROETZEL AND JIM ZIPP

NARRATIVE BY DR. ROGER J. LEDERER

First published in the United States of
America by:

Twin Lights Publishers, Inc.
8 Hale Street
Rockport, Massachusetts 01966
Telephone: (978) 546-7398
http://www.twinlightspub.com

ISBN: 1-885435-98-3
ISBN: 978-1-885435-98-9

10 9 8 7 6 5 4 3 2 1

OPPOSITE

Common Murre (*Uria aalge*)
Common Murres lay their single egg
among rocks on, or near, a cliff with no
nesting material. Unlike most birds' eggs
their egg is shaped like a top to prevent
them from rolling off the cliff. Their nesting colonies along the Atlantic coast may
number a half million birds.

FRONTISPIECE

Atlantic Puffins (*Fratercula arctica*)

JACKET FRONT

Bonaparte's Gull (*Larus philadelphia*)

JACKET BACK

Northern Parula (*Parula americana*),
Long-eared Owl (*Asio otus*),
Arctic Terns (*Sterna paradisaea*)

Book design by:
SYP Design & Production, Inc.
www.sypdesign.com

Printed in China

Over three hundred species of birds make New England their home for all or part of the year. Some are resident all year around; some come only to find a mate and raise young; a few spend only the winter here; and some just pass through on their way to other venues. This assortment of birds is made possible by the wide range of habitats in New England. Forests may be dominated by birch, hardwoods, fir, oak, or pine along with mixtures of other tree species. Riparian habitats found along streams and rivers provide different structures and food for birds, as do marshes, swamps, pastures, bogs, and meadows. Rolling hills to mountains reaching over 6000 feet and weather extremes add another level of variety. Very different environments of coastal estuaries, cliffs, and ocean waters provide yet another set of habitats for the avifauna. New England covers approximately 70,000 square miles, about 3 million square miles less than the rest of the lower 48 states, yet because of its diversity of habitats, it provides a temporary or long-term home to almost half the bird species found in North America, south of Canada.

Many birds are attractive with their colorful plumages, such as the Baltimore Oriole. Many are dainty as are the Blue-gray Gnatcatcher and classy like the Red-winged Blackbird. But even the unimaginatively named Common Grackle and Common Raven have their charms. However they are perceived by the casual observer, a closer look at any of them reveals their real appeal – their feathers, which cover virtually all of the bird. Because of their structure and the pigment they contain, feather coloration varies under different light conditions. A Blue Jay, for example, has no blue pigment, so if it stretches its wings against the light, they will appear brown. The iridescent ruby color of the Ruby-throated Hummingbird often appears to be black. Birds also have different plumages depending on their age, sex, and/or time of year. So a species of bird may be seen a hundred times before that bird truly reveals its characteristic plumage color to the observer.

To show a bird in its characteristic plumage, native habitat, and typical pose requires the utmost in photographic knowledge and skill as Jim Roetzel and Jim Zipp possess. To capture a soaring hawk, a bluebird perched on a fencepost in a meadow, or a robin yanking on a worm, the photographer also must contend with a subject that moves at its own pace, in its own light regime, often backlit against the sky. After 40 years of observing birds and looking at tens of thousands of bird photographs, I am immensely impressed by the talent these photographers have for capturing images that not only show the true color of a bird in a classic pose, but also the texture and arrangement of the feathers, eye color, and even the appearance of the bird's expression. Paraphrasing Ansel Adams, Jim Roetzel and Jim Zip do not take pictures, they make them.

OPPOSITE

Blackburnian Warbler
(*Dendroica fusca*)

Like most warblers, the Blackburnian nests in coniferous forests and forages on insects in the summer. In the winter it migrates to Central America where it will eat both insects and berries. It prefers nesting and feeding high in the trees, causing sore necks for many birdwatchers.

Bald Eagles

(*Haliaeetus leucocephalus*)

Chosen as our national symbol even though Ben Franklin preferred the Wild Turkey, the Bald Eagle was the first bird on a U.S. postage stamp. Our largest predatory bird, the wing-spread of a female can exceed seven feet. *Bald* may come from the Middle English *balled* meaning shining white or from *piebald* meaning patched.

BOTTOM

Golden Eagle

(*Aquila chrysaetos*)

Only slightly smaller, but a bit heav-ier, than the Bald Eagle and rarer in New England, the Golden Eagle subsists on prey such as rabbits, pheasants, and squirrels and can carry prey weighing as much as six pounds. They often hunt in pairs, one bird chasing the prey towards the other.

OPPOSITE

Osprey

(*Pandion haliaetus*)

Eating only fish, the Osprey has excellent eyesight, prickles on the toe bottoms, a toe that swings back-ward, and claws so long that it can-not walk. Catching fish on a third of its dives, it carries its kill head forward to reduce wind resistance. The name means *bone breaker*.

Red-shouldered Hawk
(Buteo lineatus)

This hawk with a black and white banded tail is not shy about nesting in suburbs or parks. It has a scream-like call that reminds one of a puppy whose tail was stepped on. It hunts from a perch and eats rodents, lizards, and seems to favor snakes.

Northern Goshawk
(Accipiter gentilis)

The name is derived from the old English language *GooseHawk*, although Goshawks rarely hunt geese or ducks. A fast flying bird of the forest with wide wings, which allow for maneuverability through the trees, it specializes in hunting pigeons, quail, grouse, and similar birds, often catching them in flight.

Rough-legged Hawk
(Buteo lagopus)

The name refers to the leg feathering that reaches to the toes, an adaptation to their nesting habitat in the far North. Feeding on voles and lemmings, its success on the breeding grounds in the Arctic tundra and treeless subarctic is closely tied to the availability of its prey.

Red-tailed Hawk
(Buteo jamaicensis)

The rust-colored tail is a distinguishing adult feature of the most common hawk in North America, once referred to as a *chicken hawk*. Although coloration varies from light to dark, the light chest underlined by a breast band is characteristic. Like most hawks, the female is about a third larger than the male.

Northern Harrier
(Circus cyaneus)

Once called the Marsh Hawk because of the wetland areas it inhabits, this raptor exhibits sexual dimorphism. Besides being slightly larger, the female is mainly brown while the male is mostly gray; both have distinguishing white rump patches that are easily seen as they cruise low to the ground looking for rodents.

Peregrine Falcon
(Falco peregrinus)

Once called *duck hawk*, this falcon
holds the unofficial record as the
fastest animal, cruising horizontally
at up to 70 mph and diving towards
prey at an estimated speed of up to
250 mph. Its population declined
due to DDT use, but the birds have
been recovering since the pesticide
was banned.

American Kestrel
(Falco sparverius)

The smallest of our hawks, it is actually a falcon. It looks for prey by
hovering over a likely spot and
swooping down on lizards, small
birds, and large insects. Unlike most
other birds of prey, it nests in a
cavity and both sexes share in the
incubation of the eggs.

Snowy Owl

(*Bubo scandiacus*)

The heaviest owl in North America with unmistakable white coloration and yellow eyes, it nests in the far northern edge of the Arctic, dependent largely on the fluctuating populations of lemmings. It winters as far south as the northern half of the United States where it lives on small birds and mammals.

Northern Saw-whet Owl

(*Aegolius acadicus*)

One of our smaller owls, the name comes from its call which resembles a saw being sharpened. Like all owls, it has very large eyes and exceptionally good eyesight in the dark. Its hearing is so good it can detect a beetle rustling through the leaves on the forest floor.

Long-eared Owl

(*Asio otus*)

The "ears" of this owl are feather tufts that indicate the mood of the bird, as do mammalian facial expressions, and have nothing to do with hearing. Like all owls, their wing feathers are fringed on the edges, making for silent flights as they pursue small mammals in the dark.

Barred Owl
(Strix varia)

The Barred Owl is the eastern United States counterpart of the western Spotted Owl. It calls frequently with its hoot sometimes being described as "Who cooks for you." They prefer to prey on small rodents, especially voles, but will sometimes feed on large insects.

Great Horned Owl
(Bubo virginianus)

This tufted and most widespread of all owls, with its classic hooting call, is very common throughout North America. Typical of owls, its large eyes are fixed in their sockets by a ring of bones, but they can turn their heads 270 degrees in order to see in all directions without moving their bodies.

Eastern Screech Owl
(Megascops asio)

This nocturnal bird rests during the day and to help prevent its being detected, it stretches its body so as to look like an upright branch. They regurgitate indigestible pellets containing the bones and fur or feathers of their prey; a study of these pellets can elucidate their feeding habits.

Wild Turkeys
(Meleagris gallopavo)

Native Americans ate the Wild
Turkey for hundreds of years, but by
the late 1800s they were extirpated
from New England by over hunting
and habitat loss. They have been on
the increase since being reintroduced
in the 1970s. Our domestic turkey
was bred in Europe from Wild
Turkey stock.

BOTTOM

Ring-necked Pheasant
(Phasianus colchicus)

Introduced into the United States
from its native Asia in the 1850s, the
pheasant is abundant in the northern
United States, especially in the plains
states. The colorful males are polygamous, mating with several dull colored females. Females tend to the
dozen or so eggs and young while
males defend against intruders.

OPPOSITE

Ruffed Grouse
(Bonasa umbellus)

Named because of a black "ruff" of
neck feathers that are displayed to
intruders or potential mates, the
male birds are known for a "booming" or drumming sound that accom-
panies their little show. The sounds
are actually mini sonic booms made
by quickly beating wings at five
beats per second.

Common Raven
(Corvus corax)

The largest of all songbirds, even though it only has a harsh call, it is also the most widespread of the crow and jay family. Possessing one of the largest brains in the bird world, it is generally considered the most intelligent bird and a popular subject of myths and stories.

Spruce Grouse
(Falcipennis canadensis)

Eighty percent of the grouse's year round diet is conifer needles, with the addition of berries, flowers, and invertebrates in the summer. The waxy needles are stored in the crop where digestion begins; then they move to the muscular gizzard of the stomach to be ground into pulp.

American Crow
(Corvus brachyrhynchos)

Certainly one of the most recognizable of all birds, the crow can only be confused with the raven, which is bigger and huskier than crows. For reasons yet unknown, members of the crow and jay family are especially susceptible to the West Nile Virus causing crows to die in large numbers.

PAGES 26–27 AND OPPOSITE

Eastern Bluebirds

(*Sialia sialis*)

Mainly a summer visitor to New England, bluebirds signify spring. They nest in natural tree cavities or holes made by woodpeckers in trees or fence posts. With the introduction of fiberglass fences which prevent pecking, artificial bluebird houses, such as those made by Boy Scouts, are increasingly important.

LEFT

Black-billed Cuckoo

(*Coccyzus erythropthalmus*)

Although not frequently a nest parasite and certainly not as sophisticated as its European cousin, the Black and Yellow-billed Cuckoos sometimes place their eggs in other birds' nests for those birds to raise. Cuckoos eat large numbers of tent caterpillars, destructive insects which can quickly strip deciduous trees of their leaves.

RIGHT

Indigo Bunting

(*Passerina cyanea*)

Indigo Buntings migrate to Central America and the Caribbean, traveling up to 2,000 miles or more to their wintering grounds. They migrate at night and experiments have shown that the birds use stars for navigation. Their brilliant blue color is not due to pigment but the structure of their feathers.

Yellow-breasted Chat
(*Icteria virens*)

Long considered the largest of the North American warbler family, new evidence suggests it is not a warbler at all. Its calls and songs consist of squeaks, whistles, squawks, and parts of other birds' songs. It may sing any time of day and even in the middle of the night.

Yellow-billed Cuckoo
(*Coccyzus americanus*)

The most common member of the cuckoo family in the United States (along with the Black-billed Cuckoo and Roadrunner), it arrives from its wintering grounds in South America later than most birds. It times its arrival in North America with insect outbreaks, especially caterpillars, which it regurgitates to feed its young.

Eastern Phoebe
(*Sayornis phoebe*)

Named for its call, the phoebe is one of several flycatcher species. Its lack of an eye ring distinguishes it from its cousins. Like most flycatchers, it sits on a favorite perch and sallies out to capture a flying insect; if the insect is big, it is beaten on a branch before being eaten.

White-crowned Sparrow
(*Zonotrichia leucophrys*)

Field observations of the whistling
calls of this bird have revealed that
not only do different populations
have different song accents, but so
do individual birds. Some birds can
sing or at least recognize more than
one accent. One researcher was even
able to recognize individual birds by
their songs alone.

Savannah Sparrow
(Passerculus sandwichensis)

Found all over North America, this
bird has variable characteristics and
has evolved into 17 subspecies across
its range. Recent DNA hybridization
techniques have been extremely
helpful in determining the relation-
ships of bird species. The first speci-
men collected of this species came
from Savannah, Georgia.

American Tree Sparrow
(Spizella arborea)

In spite of its name, the tree sparrow
nests on the treeless tundra and winters farther south where it forages
on the ground or in low bushes on
seeds and berries. In snowy conditions the birds will use their wings
to knock snow off grass and brush
in order to reach food.

Chipping Sparrow
(*Spizella passerina*)

A common and distinctive bird, this sparrow often lines its thin, translucent nest with horsehair, prompting some to call it *hairbird*. Typical of songbirds, it incubates its four eggs for two weeks and the young fledge ten days later. Its song, a long series of short chips, gives it its name.

Song Sparrow
(*Melospiza melodia*)

A common bird of North America, this sparrow exhibits variation in size and color. Birds in the southern part of its range are pale colored and small, and as one moves farther north, the birds become larger and darker. The streaked breast with a spot in the middle is distinctive.

Nelson's Sharp-tailed Sparrow
(*Ammodramus nelsoni*)

This sparrow is seen in New England mainly as a migrant, although some breed along the coast. Migratory birds use the day's length, not the weather, as the cue to migrate north or south. Birds arrive at their wintering or breeding destinations close to the same time each year, although weather can delay their trip.

ABOVE

American Goldfinch
(*Carduelis tristis*)

This *wild canary* is a permanent resident of New England. It eats a variety of seeds, especially thistle, and is common around winter bird feeders, usually in flocks (uncommonly called a *charm of goldfinches*). Although small, their tendency to flock and their undulating up and down flight are identifying characteristics.

OPPOSITE

Palm Warbler
(*Dendroica palmarum*)

The Palm Warbler was so named because it was first discovered on its wintering grounds in the Caribbean, but 98 percent of Palm Warblers nest in the bog forests of Canada. They nest on the ground, unusual for warblers which typically nest in trees.

European Starling
(*Sturnus vulgaris*)

European Starlings were brought to the United States in the late 1800s by those who believed all birds mentioned in Shakespeare's works ought to be imported here. They have very successfully spread across North America, displacing other birds and becoming pests in urban areas. Related to mynahs, they are good mimics.

LEFT

Bobolink

(Dolichonyx oryzivorus)

Although mainly insectivorous, they were called the *rice bird* because of their diet in the southern United States. Considered pests, they were once hunted and even shipped to New York and served in restaurants. Migration from wintering grounds in South America to their breeding grounds spans nearly 6,000 miles.

RIGHT

House Finch

(Carpodacus mexicanus)

A native of the Southwestern United States, the House Finch was imported to the East and is now found across the United States. A common visitor to bird feeders, it is bold enough to raise its young in urban and suburban areas, nesting on window sills, in flower pots, and even in garages.

TOP

Horned Lark
(*Eremophila alpestris*)

Inhabiting open country with few trees, the Horned Lark, rather than perching and singing, has a flight song which it sings while airborne. Its horns are actually small feather tufts. It is the only true lark in North America. A group of larks is uncommonly referred to as an *exaltation*.

BOTTOM LEFT

Red-winged Blackbird
(*Agelaius phoeniceus*)

The brown-streaked females are attracted to the polygamous males with a red epaulet on their black body and a distinctive call, "oh-gur-gle-eee." Experiments in which the epaulet was painted black resulted in males that were unable to defend their territory. Females choose a mate on the basis of the male's territory.

BOTTOM RIGHT

Rusty Blackbird
(*Euphagus carolinus*)

Like the Starling, the Rusty Blackbird has a *wear plumage*. In the fall its feathers are edged with a rusty brown color. By the time spring arrives the rusty brown edges will have worn off and the male birds are now ready for breeding in their glossy black plumage.

OPPOSITE

Eastern Meadowlark
(*Sturnella magna*)

Looking like it is wearing a yellow ski sweater, the warbling and melodious call of this bird is easily recognized in parks and grasslands. It overlaps in the Midwest with the virtually identical Western Meadowlark, but they do not hybridize as they have developed very different songs to distinguish themselves.

Common Grackle
(*Quiscalus quiscula*)

These iridescent black birds with a
raucous call have adapted quite well
to human disturbances and habitats.
They are abundant in suburbs, parks,
farmyards, and cemeteries. Destruction of forests has actually opened up
more habitats for these birds; their
numbers are increasing and they are
spreading westward as well.

Eastern Kingbird
(*Tyrannus tyrannus*)

Both the common name and scientific
name are derived from the aggressive
nature of this bird. Not at all shy in
defending its nest against intruders
or predators, it will attack birds considerably larger than itself. Insectivorous on its breeding grounds, it eats
mainly fruit in its wintering quarters.

TOP

Lapland Longspur
(*Calcarius lapponicus*)

In the tundra where the breeding season is short, females quickly build a nest after arriving from their wintering grounds. Incubation lasts two weeks, and the young will fledge five days after hatching, although flightless. Longspurs are named after the elongated hind toe which is advantageous in wet tundra or snow.

BOTTOM

Tree Swallow
(*Tachycineta bicolor*)

Tree Swallows nest in tree cavities or nest boxes near water. Like all swallows they are primarily insectivorous, feeding while flying, often in groups if insects are abundant. But unlike other swallows, they eat plant food such as berries and seeds if weather conditions cause a decline in flying insects.

Snow Bunting

(*Plectrophenax nivalis*)

As is the case for birds nesting in
the extreme far North, their distribution is circumpolar and they are
found in Northern Europe, Russia,
and Canada. It winters in the North
as well, farther north than any other
songbird except the Raven. Unlike
other songbirds its tarsi are feathered
for insulation.

American Robin
(*Turdus migratorius*)

The Connecticut State Bird is quintessentially American. Cocking its head as it moves across a lawn, it appears to be listening for earthworms; actually it locates them by sight but cannot see straight ahead. Although considered to be a harbinger of spring, it is a permanent resident all over the United States.

LEFT

Common Redpoll
(*Carduelis flammea*)

Redpolls are one of the birds that exhibit *irruptions* or irregular migratory movements southward during food shortages. Breeding and wintering mainly in the northern forests of Canada, the seed supply may become so depleted that the birds move into the United States, usually the only time they are seen in any numbers.

RIGHT

Northern Mockingbird
(*Mimus polyglottos*)

Mockingbirds are the most talented members of the mimic family, learning new songs throughout their life, which is unlike most birds that learn their song in their first year. Having learned perhaps 200 songs, and singing with only the light of the moon, the mockingbird is one of the more renowned birds in our gardens.

Mourning Dove
(*Zenaida macroura*)

Our most abundant and well-known native pigeon, this bird is named after its plaintive call. Like all pigeons and doves, they lay only two eggs and feed the young *pigeon milk*, actually a secretion from the lining of the crop of the parents. The parents introduce adult food slowly.

PAGES 48–49

Cedar Waxwing
(Bombycilla cedrorum)

This silky plumaged bird has secondary wing feathers which appear to have been dipped in sealing wax. A black eye mask and crest add to its identity. Berries are a favorite food and are digested in fifteen minutes. They occasionally become slightly inebriated from eating fermented berries.

ABOVE

Black-throated Blue Warbler
(Dendroica caerulescens)

Warblers are the butterflies of the bird world – flighty and flashy. The plumages of most male warblers are very colorful and boldly patterned and are sought after by birdwatchers after returning from their southern wintering grounds. Conversely, fall warblers in dull winter plumages are major challenges to birdwatchers.

Black-throated Green Warbler
(*Dendroica virens*)

Warblers are known for their complex and melodious songs. There are nearly 50 species of warblers breeding in the United States, many in the same or similar habitats, mostly that of coniferous forests. To keep the species segregated, they have evolved different characteristics in song, appearance, and sub-habitat.

ABOVE

Yellow-rumped Warbler
(*Dendroica coronata*)

One of the most common warblers,
it is one of the first to arrive from its
wintering grounds and the last to
leave. The Yellow-rumped Warbler
was created by lumping the Myrtle
Warbler (so named because it can
digest the berries of the wax-myrtle)
of the eastern United States with
the western Audubon's Warbler.

LEFT

Canada Warbler
(*Wilsonia canadensis*)

Easy to identify with a black neck-lace on a yellow body, the Canada Warbler population is declining by an estimated 4 to 7 percent per year. The bird prefers dense thickets in forests where it builds nests on the ground. Removal or thinning of undergrowth is a major reason for the population decline.

RIGHT

Nashville Warbler
(*Vermivora ruficapilla*)

It was in Nashville in the early 1800s and about the time he met Audubon for the first time in Tennessee, that Alexander Wilson, Scottish immigrant, ornithologist, naturalist, illustrator, and author of the *magnum opus*, *American Ornithology*, named this warbler. The scientific name means *red capped worm eater*.

Chestnut-sided Warbler
(*Dendroica pensylvanica*)

Two hundred years ago when North American forests were mostly virgin, these birds were scarce. With the removal of trees and the increase of second growth forests and shrubby habitat, which this species prefers, the Chestnut-sided Warbler has become one of the more abundant warblers in these habitats.

Bay-breasted Warbler
(*Dendroica castanea*)

The local population of this bird increases considerably during outbreaks of the spruce budworm, one of the most destructive pests in the spruce and fir forests of the eastern United States and Canada. Although the bird helps control the worm population, pesticides to control the worm have decreased its population.

Blue-winged Warbler
(*Vermivora pinus*)

The Blue-winged Warbler hybridizes with the Golden-winged Warbler in the east central United States, resulting in a variety of color patterns. This intermixing of species questions whether these two birds are actually true and separate species, although the Blue-winged Warbler appears to be displacing its counterpart.

OPPOSITE

Yellow-bellied Sapsucker
(*Sphyrapicus varius*)

The sapsucker is a woodpecker, common in the eastern United States. It is best known for drilling a series of small holes in trees, causing them to exude sap. Using their brushy tongue, they lap up the sap and eat the insects that are drawn to it.

ABOVE

Hooded Warbler
(*Wilsonia citrina*)

Like other songbirds, the Hooded Warbler establishes a territory in which the pair builds a nest and raise their young. DNA studies have shown that one third of the young in females' nests are fathered not by the territory owner but by a neighboring male.

Blackburnian Warbler

(*Dendroica fusca*)

Named after an 18th-century English botanist, Anna Blackburne, its genus name *Dendroica* means tree dweller, which is certainly characteristic of most warblers. The Blackburnian feeds on tree tops and nests high in coniferous trees of northeastern North America. Its spectacular colors belie its species name *fusca*, meaning *dusky*.

American Redstart
(*Setophaga ruticilla*)

A little more than five inches long and weighing about as much as eight paperclips, this warbler is noticeable in both plumage and behavior. The bird often jumps or flies and captures insects in midair. It often wags its patterned tail in display while on the ground or in a low bush.

Black-and-White Warbler

(*Mniotilta varia*)

This is the only warbler that commonly forages on tree trunks and limbs, hugging the bark. Its slightly longer and downcurved bill probes the crevices of the bark for insects, larvae, and eggs. The toes have long claws for holding onto bark and the hind toe is distinctly longer than other warblers'.

Wilson's Warbler

(*Wilsonia pusilla*)

Named by Alexander Wilson after himself, this is a bird of thickets, mainly in wet habitats. Between breeding, migration, and wintering areas, this bird is found all over North America. Because of the disappearance of riparian habitats in some parts of the country, this species is one of concern.

Mourning Warbler

(*Oporornis philadelphia*)

Rather than a plaintive call, this bird gets its name either from the gray hood or from the black patch on the upper chest, each presumably a symbol of mourning. The species name refers to the city in which Alexander Wilson first saw the bird; few are seen there now.

Northern Parula

(*Parula americana*)

Pronounced *PAR-u-la* or *PAR-you-la* or *PAIR-u-la*, the name means *little titmouse* as it is a small warbler that behaves a bit like a titmouse. It nests high in trees, preferring to use lichens or Spanish moss for a nest site. Although an eastern United States bird, vagrants have shown up as far west as California.

White-eyed Vireo
(*Vireo griseus*)

This bird, being rather cryptically colored is more often detected by its song than sight. It is a distinctive and complex song, easily distinguished from others and is sometimes described as "chick-per-a-weeo" or "chick-per-a-weeo-chick." Learning song mnemonics such as these can be very helpful in identifying birds.

Ruby-crowned Kinglet
(*Regulus calendula*)

A flighty, tiny bird with dull green coloration, it flashes a ruby red head patch when excited. Both male and female build a hanging cup nest, built of moss and spider webs, and lined with feathers. As many as 12 eggs can be laid, their total weight exceeding that of the female.

Ruby-throated Hummingbird
(*Archilochus colubris*)

The only hummingbird of the eastern United States, this tiny bird flies 500 miles non-stop across the Yucatan Peninsula from its wintering grounds. Able to sop up nectar from flowers or hummer feeders with its mop-like tongue, it feeds on insects during breeding season because their young need protein to grow.

Veery
(*Catharus fuscescens*)

These thrushes are found in hard-wood and mixed forests with a dense understory. They forage by flipping over leaves, looking for invertebrates or berries, and they may make short sorties to catch flying insects. Their vision in low light is exceptionally good and they migrate at night, as do all thrushes.

Purple Finch
(*Carpodacus purpureus*)

The New Hampshire State Bird is really a dark rose color. It is being displaced by the very adaptable and unfussy House Finch, similar in color but a brighter red, and by the ubiqui-tous House Sparrow. Their simple nest, usually in a coniferous tree, may be used for several years.

Warbling Vireo

(Vireo gilvus)

Although its breeding range is the entire United States and the western half of Canada, this bird is more often heard than seen. The male sings its complicated song from the nest and it sounds like, "If I sees you; I will seize you; and I'll squeeze you till you squirt."

Winter Wren

(Troglodytes troglodytes)

A *troglodyte* is a cave dweller. In the winter these birds huddle together in a cavity in a tree or old nest. During breeding season, the male may build several nests before a female finds one she likes. The unused nests may be abandoned or used for another breeding attempt.

Eastern Wood Pewee

(Contopus virens)

Like the phoebe, the pewee name comes not from its size but its call, "pee-oh-wee." This flycatcher's call is heard more often than the birds are observed because of their dull gray coloration and tendency to inhabit the higher reaches of the forest canopy where it builds a cryptic nest.

TOP

White-winged Crossbill
(Loxia leucoptera)

The purpose of the crossed tips of the bill is to pry open coniferous cones such as spruce and larch in order to get at the seeds. The bills may cross in either direction, but that direction determines which way the bird will spiral up the cone as it looks for seeds.

BOTTOM

Pine Grosbeak
(Pinicola enucleator)

These largest of northern finches are often seen in large flocks in the winter. They are not frightened easily and can be closely approached. They are especially striking in the winter when the bright red males are seen against the white snow. They were depicted on the 1986 Canadian $1,000 bill.

OPPOSITE

Red Crossbill
(Loxia curvirostra)

There are at least nine populations of Red Crossbills which can only be distinguished by analyzing their calls. Their colors vary from yellowish to red, depending on the levels of red pigment they ingest. They may breed any time of year as their breeding cycles are heavily dependent on food supplies.

OPPOSITE

Black-capped Chickadee
(*Poecile atricapillus*)

This familiar bird gets its name from its "chick-a-dee-dee-dee" call. This call has been found to be very complex as variations in it serve to communicate with mates, coordinate flocks in the winter, or warn against predators; in the latter case extra "dees" are added to the end.

TOP

Yellow Warbler
(*Dendroica petechia*)

Popular with birdwatchers because of their bright coloration and lovely song, this yellowest of all warblers is found throughout North America in riparian vegetation. Their populations are overall stable but declining in some areas due to removal of willows and nest parasitism by the Brown-headed Cowbird.

BOTTOM

White-throated Sparrow
(*Zonotrichia albicollis*)

Another bird with a call easily remembered by a mnemonic, this bird says "Poor Sam Peabody, Peabody, Peabody." These birds have two color phases, tan and white. Research shows that the somewhat shy tan birds nest in low density areas while more aggressive white birds nest in high density ones.

Rose-breasted Grosbeak
(*Pheucticus ludovicianus*)

The female, resembling a large sparrow, sports a much different plumage
than the stunning male Rose-breasted Grosbeak, which is black, white,
and red-rose. Why? Because the
male has to attract a mate and protect the territory while the female
has to be cryptic as she tends to
parental duties.

OPPOSITE

Evening Grosbeak
(*Coccothraustes vespertinus*)

The scientific name of this bird
means *seed breaker of the evening*, describ-
ing the common name given to it by
early French Canadian pioneers. Its
heavy bill reflects its ability to crack
open hard seeds and nuts, exerting
up to 150 pounds per square inch,
enough to split a cherry pit.

LEFT

Blue-gray Gnatcatcher
(Polioptila caerulea)

This active, small gray bird with
a long black tail, which is often
cocked, resembles a miniature mockingbird. In eastern North America
it prefers moist deciduous woodlands where it gleans insects and
larvae off of branches and leaves or
flushes insects and snaps them up
on short sallies.

RIGHT

Common Nighthawk
(Chordeiles minor)

Active at dawn and dusk, the nighthawk captures insects while flying by
opening its amazingly large mouth
that has sticky surfaces to which the
insects adhere. It is sometimes called
the "bullbat" because of its habit of
swooping down from great heights
and opening its wings near the
ground, making a booming sound.

OPPOSITE

Eastern Towhee
(Pipilo erythrophthalmus)

"Drink your tea, drink your tea" is
more often heard than this pretty
bird is seen because of its tendency
to perch in dense brush, although it
is common around human habita-
tion. It commonly feeds on the
ground where it scratches for food,
sometimes with both feet at once.

TOP

Great Crested Flycatcher
(*Myiarchus crinitus*)

One characteristic of flycatchers is the crest that is raised or lowered depending on their mood, but it is not always present. These large flycatchers can sometimes be heard snapping their triangular and slightly hooked bills together as they attempt to capture insects in mid-air.

BOTTOM

Yellow-bellied Flycatcher
(*Empidonax flaviventris*)

Although this photo shows a distinctively yellowish bird, the Yellow-bellied Flycatcher sometimes only shows a subtle wash of yellow. Flycatchers of the genus *Empidonax* are notoriously hard to tell apart, even during breeding season, and a patient observer must use habitat, song, and plumage combinations to do so.

LEFT

Willow Flycatcher
(*Empidonax traillii*)

As is characteristic of all *Empidonax* flycatchers, the Willow Flycatcher shows the white eye ring and white wing bars. Similar in behavior as well, they sit straight up and often flick their tails and wings. Populations of this bird are declining and the southwestern subspecies is on the endangered list.

RIGHT

Acadian Flycatcher
(*Empidonax virescens*)

When three or four flycatchers inhabit the same geographical area and habitat, they segregate themselves by feeding and nesting at different heights and horizontal locations in the vegetation. They do this to lessen competition for similar resources. All flycatchers winter in Mexico, or Central or South America.

Brown Thrasher
(*Toxostoma rufum*)

A large bird with a long tail, it is secretive and heard more often than seen as it *thrashes* the leaf litter in search of crickets, grasshoppers, worms, berries, and nuts. A mimic related to the mockingbird, it repeats every note twice while the mockingbird repeats them three times.

Purple Martins
(*Progne subis*)

Birdhouses have been erected for Purple Martins for many years and in some areas of the country they nest nowhere else. Martins have a reputation of being prodigious consumers of mosquitoes, however, this is not true. Instead, they catch insects while in flight during the daylight while mosquitoes stay in low dark places.

Dark-eyed Junco

(*Junco hyemalis*)

Once thought to be several species, it in fact shows much variability in coloration and pattern. All have white outer tail feathers, which are usually only seen in flight, the purpose being they might be a distraction for a predator as the white feathers fold under the gray feathers upon landing.

Tufted Titmouse

(*Baeolophus bicolor*)

The Tufted Titmouse, although plainly colored, has an erect crest and a call of "Peter, Peter, Peter" that easily distinguishes it. Common in woodlands, parks, and backyards where it nests in cavities, its range is moving northward due to an increase in bird feeders and/or warming of the climate.

LEFT TOP

Marsh Wren
(Cistothorus palustris)

Marsh Wrens feed on insects from stems of dense marsh vegetation, the ground, or the water's surface. Secretive, they only pop into view occasionally. Marsh Wrens build oval nests with side entrances and may build an additional dozen or more incomplete nests, perhaps to avoid predators or for additional shelters.

LEFT BOTTOM

Red-eyed Vireo
(Vireo olivaceus)

Red-eyed Vireos were once thought to be one of the three most abundant birds in the eastern deciduous forest, but habitat destruction and nest parasitism have taken a toll. The population of this species suffers from nest parasitism by the Brown-headed Cowbird.

RIGHT

House Wren
(Troglodytes aedon)

The House Wren nests in natural cavities or nest boxes in many habitats. They prefer open areas and studies have shown that they have more success defending their nests when they are located in sparse vegetation.

Gray Catbird
(*Dumetella carolinensis*)

Another relative of the mocking
bird, it has a large repertoire of
songs, but does not repeat itself as
do the mockingbird and thrasher. It
also makes a sound reminiscent of a
cat. Like the mockingbird, it has
adapted well to humans and is common in suburban areas and parks.

Hermit Thrush
(Catharus guttatus)

The Hermit Thrush does not leave North America for the winter like other thrushes; it simply changes its diet by adding more berries and eating fewer insects. The Vermont State Bird, *thrush* derives from the Middle English *thrusche*, meaning cheerful person and probably pertaining to the bird's song.

Northern Waterthrush
(Seiurus noveboracensis)

This bird is actually a warbler that acts and looks more like a small thrush. Brown with a spotted white breast, it walks slowly over the ground in search of food items. Except for New England and the Great Lakes states, the lower United States sees this bird only during migration.

Ovenbird
(Seiurus aurocapillus)

Another warbler, closely related to the waterthrushes, it gets its name from its domed nest of twigs and grass with a side entrance that resembles a miniature clay oven. It is well known for its call of "teacher, teacher, teacher" while it walks alone on the moist forest floor.

Pine Siskin
(Carduelis pinus)

Siskin is a word derived from the Dutch and refers to the call of these thin-billed, sparrow-like birds. Brown streaked and with distinctive yellow wing patches, they feed on seeds and often hang upside down to do so. Hanging feeders used for goldfinches and nuthatches will attract these birds as well.

Baltimore Oriole

(*Icterus galbula*)

The name *Baltimore* derives from Baron Baltimore of Ireland whose descendents were the proprietors of the former Province of Maryland. *Oriole* derives from their appearance to tropical orioles. Maryland's state bird, North American orioles are closely related to blackbirds. Open area inhabitants, they eat fruit and insects.

Common Yellowthroat

(*Geothylpis trichas*)

These birds typically frequent cattail marshes and other wetlands with dense growth, feeding on insects and sometimes small seeds. They are a species of warbler that sometimes cock their tails up like wrens, and are easily recognized by their "whichity, whichity, whichity" call and their black face mask over a yellow throat.

White-breasted Nuthatch

(*Sitta carolinensis*)

Flying to the upper trunk of a tree, the nuthatch works its way downward, head first, searching for insects in the crevices of the bark. It also collects seeds and nuts, wedges them into crevices and returns at a later date to eat them, *hatching* them by breaking their shells.

LEFT

Northern Cardinal
(*Cardinalis cardinalis*)

Unmistakable with his bright red plumage, black face, and topknot, the male Northern Cardinal is non-migratory. The familiar whistling call is often described as "pretty, pretty, pretty." Cardinals are known for attacking their reflection in windows and car mirrors, supposedly defending their territory against intruders.

RIGHT

Scarlet Tanager
(*Piranga olivacea*)

There are 240 species of tanagers, all but five restricted to Central and South America. Very brightly colored birds, their cone shaped beak allows them to eat a variety of foods, especially fruit and insects. The brilliant Scarlet Tanager is secretive and prefers to inhabit the high canopy in dense forests.

Blue Jay
(Cyanocitta cristata)

The Blue Jay is known for its bold contrasting coloration, head crest, and distinctive "Jaay, Jaay" call. The blue hue of its feathers is a result of light refraction rather than pigmentation. Catholic in its food and habitat preferences, its migratory habits are also flexible; it may migrate one year and not the next.

OPPOSITE

Gray Jay
(Perisoreus canadensis)

Found all over Canada, the Gray Jay is restricted to far northern New England. Rather than migrating, it caches its food, insects, spiders, berries, and mushrooms (not seeds, surprisingly) by gluing food items with its sticky saliva to tree branches high enough so they will not be covered by snow.

ABOVE

Blue-headed Vireo
(Vireo solitarius)

What was once called the Solitary Vireo was discovered via molecular genetic studies to actually be three species: the Plumbeous, the Cassins, and the Blue-headed Vireo. Vireos resemble warblers, live in similar habitats, and are also insectivorous but they are more deliberate in their movements and less colorful.

Pileated Woodpecker

(*Dryocopus pileatus*)

Whether pronounced *Pill-eated* or *Pile-eated* (referring to the bird's crest) this largest of United States woodpeckers, and the model for the Woody Woodpecker character, is sometimes mistaken for the extinct Ivory-billed Woodpecker. An excavator of tree holes, it has bristles over its nostrils to keep out wood chips.

Northern Flicker

(*Colaptes auratus*)

With yellow underwings and a white rump, this common woodpecker of backyards and open woods prefers to feed on the ground. They are sometimes seen rubbing ants through their feathers, a behavior known as anting, which uses the formic acid from the ants to kill feather parasites. Males have a red or yellow mustache.

Belted Kingfisher
(*Megaceryle alcyon*)

Found perched along watercourses, this bird is the only common king-fisher in the United States that dives for fish, returns to its perch, and hits the fish against the perch to stun it. They build their nests in a stream bank burrow which they excavate with the help of partially fused toes.

LEFT

Hairy Woodpecker
(Picoides villosus)

In order to climb trees and peck wood, woodpeckers have two toes in front and back and stiffened tail feathers. In order to reach far into tree bark crevices for insects, the sticky tongue is supported by a long y-shaped bone that wraps over the back of the skull.

RIGHT

Downy Woodpecker
(Picoides pubescens)

Downy and Hairy Woodpeckers are very similar except that the Downy is smaller and has a short stubby bill. They are found in the same habitats and in order to minimize competition, the Hairy searches for insects on the trunk and larger branches while the Downy restricts itself to smaller ones.

OPPOSITE

Red-bellied Woodpecker
(Melanerpes carolinus)

Seemingly misnamed, there is a reddish tinge on the lower belly. Like all woodpeckers, they chip away at trees for food and to make cavities for their nest. Their drumming on a tree, fence post, or house siding is for communication and is as distinctive as their calls.

Snow Geese
(*Chen caerulescens*)

Seen only on migration and on their wintering grounds in parts of New England, their name comes from the view one gets when observing great numbers of Snow Geese coming in for a landing, like a snowfall. There is also an alternate form called the *blue goose*, although it is actually gray.

TOP

Canvasback
(*Aythya valisineria*)

Most ducks are divided into one of two groups: dabbling or diving. The Canvasback is a diver and eats aquatic plants, snails, insects, and small fish. Besides being reddish, the sloping profile of its head is a good identifying characteristic as it can only be confused with the Redhead (duck).

BOTTOM

Common Goldeneye
(*Bucephala clangula*)

Found year-round in northern New England and wintering elsewhere in the area, goldeneyes breed in the coniferous forests of Canada. They make their nests in tree cavities, formed either by broken off limbs or by Pileated Woodpeckers. Both male and female adults have bright, golden-yellow eyes.

96

ABOVE

Harlequin Ducks
(*Histrionicus histrionicus*)

A sea duck seen only in the winter along the coast, it is named after a colorfully dressed comic character in Italian theater. In spring they leave their salt water habitats and move to fast moving streams to breed. They are sometimes called *lords and ladies*, *painted ducks*, and *totem pole ducks*.

TOP

Surf Scoter

(Melanitta perspicillata)

Breeding only in far north Canada and Alaska, they are only seen in New England on migration and in the winter along the coast. Their bulky head and white head patches distinguish these sea birds which are named for their inclination to forage in the surf and breaking waves.

BOTTOM LEFT

Mallard

(Anas platyrhynchos)

The most familiar of all ducks and found throughout the Northern Hemisphere, it has given rise to almost all of our domestic ducks. Like all ducks, courtship occurs on the fall wintering grounds and the pair fly north to raise their brood; the cryptic-colored female doing all the domestic work.

BOTTOM RIGHT

Redhead

(Aythya americana)

With a rusty red head and coloration that matches that of the Canvasback, the Redhead, also a diver, has a more typical head shape. Ninety percent of its diet is vegetation. Its breeding habits seem rather casual as the Redhead female often lays her eggs in the nest of other birds.

Ruddy Duck
(*Oxyura jamaicensis*)

This bird belongs to the family of *stiff-tailed* ducks and its erect fan-shaped tail attests to that. Occasionally called *blue bill* because of its bluish beak, it dives for aquatic vegetation, seeds, and invertebrates. It is often a *brood parasite* like the Redhead and lays its eggs in other ducks' nests.

OPPOSITE

Red-throated Loon
(*Gavia stellata*)

The smallest of the five North American loons, it is found in New England only on the coast during the winter. *Loon* comes from the Norwegian *lom* meaning *clumsy person*, as the legs, webbed and located far back on the body, are great for swimming but make walking extremely awkward.

TOP

Common Loon
(*Gavia immer*)

With its eerie call, this large black-and-white bird symbolizes the far North. Found in the Northeast all year and on coastal waters during the winter, they build mound nests very close to the water, and after hatching the young ride upon the back of the parents until they become independent.

BOTTOM

Wood Duck
(*Aix sponsa*)

Ducks are sexually dimorphic, which simply means that the males and females look different. It couldn't be truer for the Wood Duck as the male is spectacularly colored and patterned while the mainly brown female pales in comparison. The colors reflect their roles in nature: attract a mate or raise young.

Brant

(Branta bernicla)

An attractive, fast-flying, small goose, almost duck size, the Brant nests in the extreme North and winters along the coastline where it subsists on eelgrass. Its name is apparently derived from its call, although the Brant is also called the Black Brant and referred to as the Brent in Britain.

Northern Shoveler

(Anas clypeata)

Seen only on migration, the shoveler has a spoon-like bill with fine bristle-like projections to filter out food that it picks up from the water using a side-to-side head movement. Resembling a mallard with its green head, it is sometimes called *Hollywood Mallard, Laughing Mallard,* or *Daffy Duck* by hunters.

Northern Pintail

(Anas acuta)

Seen in the winter, the fast flying pintail shows a streamlined aerodynamic silhouette. Like all ducks after mating and the females begin their domestic duties, the males quickly lose their mating plumage and take on a flightless female-looking *eclipse* plumage until fall when they don their courtship colors once more.

Common Merganser

(*Mergus merganser*)

Birds do not have teeth, but mergansers have the next best thing, a serrated bill with which to snag fish. Often seen on rivers and lakes, they will also feed on frogs and large insects. Diving birds, their common name comes from the Latin *mergus* (diver) and *anser* (goose).

American Wigeon
(Anas americana)

Because of the wide white stripe on the male's head, this duck was once known as the *baldpate*. A higher percentage of its diet is vegetation, compared to other ducks, and its short bill allows it to exert more force in dislodging and chewing vegetation than other dabbling ducks.

American Black Duck
(Anas rubripes)

The American Black Duck male looks like a female Mallard and indeed, it is related to the Mallard, with which it interbreeds. As is true with many ducks, there is a patch of iridescent feathers on the back of the wing called a *speculum*, which is important in identification of several species.

Red-breasted Merganser
(Mergus serrator)

These birds build a roofed nest lined with grass and feathers and lay 9 to 10 and even up to 24 eggs. If predators destroy the eggs, the parents may renest. Young from several broods may join to form large aggregations which are typically attended by only one female.

Blue-winged Teals

(*Anas discors*)

One clue to identifying teal is their
small size and fast flight and their
habitat on bays, ponds, and marshes.
The male duck peeps loudly while
the female softly peeps. Both have
a blue area on the forward edge of
their wings and the male has a white
crescent on the face.

Bufflehead

(*Bucephala albeola*)

Tree nesters, they often use holes made by the Northern Flicker because they are too small for other ducks. Pairs may stay together only one season, but the female may use the same nest hole for several years. The name is a contraction of *buffalo head*, a reference to their head shape.

Common Eider

(*Somateria mollissima*)

Eiders are the heaviest ducks in North America. They are harvested in Iceland for their down, which is highly valued as the lightest and most effective insulating material. The down is collected from the nests and not from the birds, so the feathers can be collected without harm to the adults or young.

TOP

Horned Grebe
(Podiceps auritus)

In breeding season, yellow feather plumes over the ears give this bird its name. But in the winter, along the New England coast, it can only be identified by its black and white plumage, red eye, and diving behavior. They seldom fly on their wintering grounds and migrate only at night.

BOTTOM

Red-necked Grebes
(Podiceps grisegena)

Of the seven species of grebes in the United States this is the second largest. It winters on the coast. During migration, it sticks to the coast during the day but at night it flies over land. It eats feathers, as do all grebes, to protect the stomach from fish bones.

ABOVE

Pied-billed Grebe
(Podilymbus podiceps)

Pied means *patched* and refers to the black band on the white bill. Rarely seen flying, these birds prefer to dunk beneath the water when disturbed. Like other grebes, the newly hatch young ride on the back of the parents until independent although they can swim almost immediately after hatching.

TOP
Long-tailed Ducks
(Clangula byemalis)

Once called the old squaw, this duck was hunted in great numbers in the early 1900s for its thick down which was stuffed into pillows. Like most ducks, the female lines the nest with this wonderful insulation. Unlike other ducks, the Long-tailed Duck undergoes three, not two, molts per year.

BOTTOM
Common Murre
(Uria aalge)

Common Murres lay their single egg among rocks on or near a cliff with no nesting material. Unlike most birds' eggs theirs is top-shaped to prevent them from rolling off the cliff. This photo shows the winter plumage and the far rearward place-ment of their legs, well suited for diving.

OPPOSITE
Thick-billed Murre
(Uria lomvia)

Nesting in the far Arctic around the world, Thick-billed Murres feed on fish, squid, and other invertebrates, flying as far as 60 miles from their nest sites and diving as deep as 600 feet in the sea. They only lay one egg and surround it with pebbles to make a nest.

TOP

Ring-necked Duck
(Aythya collaris)

The brownish ring around its neck is difficult to see against the black plumage of the male. Ring-billed Duck would be a more appropriate appellation. The dull brown female builds a nest on a small island or on floating vegetation, laying 6–14 eggs that take nearly a month to hatch.

BOTTOM

Greater Scaups
(Aythya marila)

The Lesser and Greater Scaup are difficult to distinguish from each other, but large concentrations of birds on the Northeast coast are almost certainly the Greater, which is the slightly larger and heavier species. They dive for mussels, shrimp, fish, and small portions of plant material.

OPPOSITE

Atlantic Puffins
(Fratercula arctica)

A colorful and popular bird, the Atlantic Puffin is a prodigious fish eater. Although its colorful bill does not seem to be shaped for fishing, the birds, with backward projecting spines on their tongue, can catch, hold, and fly back to their nest with dozens of small fish in their beak.

OPPOSITE
Razorbill
(Alca torda)

The Razorbill belongs to the auk family, which includes puffins, murres, and auks. Penguin-like, they are actually more related to shorebirds. Their wings are adapted for both aerial and *underwater flying*. Their year is spent on the open ocean except during breeding season when they nest on cliffs or in burrows.

TOP
Double-crested Cormorant
(Phalacrocorax auritus)

This aquatic fish-eater is named for the feather tufts on the sides of its head. Of the six species of cormorants in North America, this is the only one found far inland. Not sanitary, it may incorporate plastic, paper, and bones into its nest, and not clean it as most birds do.

BOTTOM
Canada Goose
(Branta canadensis)

Our most abundant and well-known goose, Canada Goose numbers are increasing and it is considered a pest in some areas such as parks and golf courses due to its aggressiveness and droppings. Calling it a *Canadian Goose* is a common misnomer because all North American geese nest in Canada.

Sora

(Porzana carolina)

The Sora is the most common of all North American rails but not often seen because, like all rails, it is secretive and restricts itself to running through its marshy habitat. It can maneuver between rushes and cattails because it is laterally flattened, giving us the phrase *skinny as a rail*.

Clapper Rail

(Rallus longirostris)

The Clapper Rail is fairly common but with a discontinuous distribution along the United States coast where it inhabits salt marshes and mangrove swamps. It detects its food of invertebrates by probing in the muck or catching fish and crayfish by sight. It hybridizes with the very similar King Rail.

Virginia Rail

(Rallus limicola)

The rails are related to cranes, coots, and gallinules, all of which inhabit wetland areas. Rails frequent every continent except Antarctica and many islands; several island forms are flightless. The secretive Virginia Rail, most active at dusk and dawn, is not only shy and avoids flying, it can also swim underwater.

TOP
Mute Swan
(*Cygnus olor*)

The largest waterfowl in North America, the Mute Swan is native to Europe and was introduced into the eastern United States in the late 19th century. Since then its numbers have increased and due to its size and aggressiveness it has been outcompeting other waterfowl for food and nesting sites.

BOTTOM
Gadwall
(*Anas strepera*)

The Gadwall is a dabbling duck that tips forward and dips its head into the water. It then sucks water in and ejects it out the sides of its bill, straining out food with ridges called lamellae. Helping to detect the food items, the edges of a duck's bill have tactile receptors.

American Coot
(*Fulica americana*)

Related to rails, the black coot stands out from the ducks it is often found alongside. The atypical, white bill is small and laterally flattened. Its toes are not webbed but lobed. A weak flier with a large dumpy body, it can easily walk and run on land.

PAGES 120–121 AND TOP

Arctic Terns
(*Sterna paradisaea*)

A standout in the bird world because of its incredible annual migratory journey, the Arctic Tern makes a 24,000 mile round trip from its breeding grounds in the circum-polar Arctic to its wintering grounds in the Antarctic. It most likely is exposed to more daylight than any other animal.

BOTTOM AND OPPOSITE

Common Terns
(*Sterna hirundo*)

Terns dive into the water with pointed bills to catch their fish or shrimp prey. They are narrow-winged, streamlined and graceful, reflected by the scientific name of the Common Tern which means *sea swallow*. Nearly all are seabirds but the Common Tern is widespread and found far inland in North America.

ABOVE AND OPPOSITE

Herring Gulls
(Larus argentatus)

Although no bird is technically named *seagull*, this very common gull fits that description. It takes four years for a Herring Gull to don its adult plumage, but it may live for over 30 years. Young Herring Gull chicks peck at the red spot on the parent's bill to stimulate them to regurgitate food.

TOP

Parasitic Jaeger
(*Stercorarius parasiticus*)

Also called the Arctic Skua, these visitors from the Arctic usually arrive in New England waters in July. Their name comes from their habit of *kleptoparasitism* as they often harass gulls and terns to make them drop their prey or even regurgitate stomach contents.

BOTTOM LEFT

Lesser Black-backed Gull
(*Larus fuscus*)

Gulls, unlike terns, are heavier bodied with a slightly hooked upper bill. They do not dive but are opportunistic feeders on a variety of foods and are common on garbage piles. This photo shows a bird in its third winter plumage, about to molt into its adult feathers.

BOTTOM RIGHT

Bonaparte's Gull
(*Larus philadelphia*)

More tern-like than other gulls, the Bonaparte's has a thin bill and tern-like flight. It nests in trees while other gulls regularly nest on the ground. It was named after a nephew of Napoleon who was a zoologist. The species' scientific name comes from the site of its first collection and description.

Black Skimmers
(*Rynchops niger*)

The three species of skimmer in the world feed in a unique manner: they fly over saltwater with their lower mandible skimming through the first inch or two of the surface. When a prey is encountered, they snap it up. Since sight is not essential, they most often feed at night.

ABOVE

Laughing Gulls
(*Larus atricilla*)

This common coastal bird is named for its laughing call. It is an excellent swimmer with its webbed feet but rarely submerges. Particularly bold birds, as are most gulls, they can be seen begging at beaches for hand-outs and following fishing trawlers for scraps. They nest in colonies, laying four eggs.

OPPOSITE

Northern Gannets
(*Morus bassanus*)

This seabird may dive from 100 feet with its wings swept back in search of prey. As adaptations for diving, it has air cells under the skin around its neck and shoulders, no nostrils, and can swim a short distance under-water. Gannets mate for life, using the same nest each year.

PAGES 130–131 AND OPPOSITE

Great Egrets
(Ardea alba)

Found all over the world and most of the United States, this large white bird is very common in wetlands and much larger than the Snowy or Cattle Egrets. There is no difference between herons and egrets; the name *heron* was derived from the German and *egret* from the French.

LEFT
Cattle Egret
(Bubulcus ibis)

The Cattle Egret is the only common bird in North America that introduced itself to the continent rather than relying on humans to do so. It apparently flew across the Atlantic to South America from its home in the Old World over a hundred years ago and has been moving northward across the United States ever since.

RIGHT
Snowy Egret
(Egretta thula)

Once hunted for their showy plumes worth more per ounce than gold, egrets were brought to the brink of extinction by milliners dealing in ornate and fanciful headwear. Although egret feathers were most popular, the feathers of dozens of bird species were used this way in the 19th and early 20th centuries.

OPPOSITE

Glossy Ibises

(Plegadis falcinellus)

An unmistakable bird with its glossy purplish plumage and long down-curved bill, the Glossy Ibis is very nomadic and may be abundant in an area one year and absent the next. It prefers freshwater habitats where it feeds on invertebrates such as worms, crayfish, and insects with its sensitive, sickle-shaped bill.

TOP

Sandhill Crane

(Grus canadensis)

Although Sandhill Cranes are the most common crane in the world, they are extremely rare in New England. There is a record of one pair recently breeding in Maine, yet there may be others. Evidence indicates that Sandhills frequented New England a hundred and more years ago but unexplainably disappeared.

BOTTOM

Hudsonian Godwit

(Limosa haemastica)

Traveling from the far north Arctic breeding grounds to their wintering quarters in Patagonia, godwits give New Englanders only a short window of opportunity to observe them on their migration along the coast. The long bill can be opened only at the tip, allowing them to probe deeper than other shorebirds.

Least Bittern

(*Ixobrychus exilis*)

While the heron and egret names derive from German and French, *bittern* derives from old English. The smallest of the heron family, they nest in freshwater marshes and swamps. These low flying birds sometimes meet their demise by hitting power lines, windows, or automobiles.

American Bittern

(*Botaurus lentiginosus*)

The streaked body and stiff, still posture of the American Bittern camouflage it well in dense marshy vegetation, only revealing itself at the last minute with a frantic burst of flight. Its unusual call carries far and sounds like a plunger or pump, giving the bird an alternative name of *bog pumper*.

Little Blue Heron

(*Egretta caerulea*)

This heron stands quietly in the water and waits for crayfish, fish, frogs, snakes, insects, or other prey to swim by and then quickly snaps them up. The bird will also follow farm machinery and preys on the flushed animals. Adults are bluish gray but young birds are white.

Green Heron

(*Butorides virescens*)

Green Herons are common yet small and secretive. Living along the waters' edge of forests, they have a slow, deliberate walk and an elaborate set of body postures and movements. These gestures communicate information to mates, territory intruders, and other birds as a warnings that a predator is approaching.

Great Blue Herons

(*Ardea herodias*)

Common throughout the United States, this tall bird stands in or near water and spears fish and frogs and also snatches crayfish, snakes, insects, and mice. Its ungainly flight makes it appear to some as a prehistoric creature.

Tricolored Heron
(Egretta tricolor)

The only heron with white markings on the front, this bird was formerly known as the Louisiana Heron. Often standing belly-deep in water, it may run quickly through the shallows with bent legs and raised wings, looking for prey. At times it will extend a foot forward and vibrate it to flush prey.

Yellow-crowned Night-Heron
(Nyctanassa violacea)

The Black-crowned Night-Heron is found over most of the United States but the Yellow-crowned is restricted to the East. They build a nest of sticks in a tree and their three to five eggs hatch in about three weeks. The parents partially digest the food and regurgitate it to the young.

Black-crowned Night-Heron
(Nycticorax nycticorax)

As their name suggests, this heron, more widespread in the world than other herons, is mainly nocturnal. To attract females and express displeasure to competitors, the male walks around, hunched over, and snaps its bill vigorously. After the male and female pair up, they preen each other to cement their relationship.

SHOREBIRDS

Ruddy Turnstones

(Arenaria interpres)

This shorebird breeds in the far North and winters on the southern New England coast. As the name suggests, they roll over stones looking for prey, mostly invertebrates, but will eat almost anything, even carrion. The pattern of black, white, and ruddy red coloration and yellow legs are distinctive.

Red-necked Phalarope

(Phalaropus lobatus)

The phalarope has lobed feet and swims in tight circles to stir up prey. It is unusual in its reversed sexual dimorphism—the female is brightly colored while the male is dull. This is because the gender roles are also reversed—the males, rather than females, incubate the eggs and guard the young.

Short-billed Dowitcher

(Limnodromus griseus)

Shorebirds possess a wide variety of bills from long to short, and straight, downcurved, or recurved. These variations allow the birds, who all feed in similar wet environments, to eat different foods by skimming off the water's surface or probing to different depths. *Dowitcher* is a Native American word.

Semipalmated Plover
(*Charadrius semipalmatus*)

There are a few dozen birds in the plover family across the globe, many having some sort of breast band and all having a swollen bill tip. *Plover* comes from the old English or French and refers to rain. Semipalmated refers to a partial webbing of the toes, helpful in locomotion.

TOP

Sanderling
(Calidris alba)

A widespread and common shorebird worldwide, its white undersides, black legs, and habit of following and chasing the surf along the beach characterize this sandpiper. It is the only one without a rear toe, supposedly an adaptation for running. In flight, the white wing stripe bordered by black is visible.

BOTTOM

Piping Plover
(Charadrius melodus)

Common along the Atlantic coast during the 19th century, Piping Plovers were hunted for hat decorations, which nearly brought them to extinction. The Migratory Bird Treaty Act of 1918 allowed plovers to recover and their population peaked in the 1940s.

American Golden-Plover
(*Pluvialis dominica*)

Having attained a substantial layer of fat beforehand, the American Golden-Plover migrates from the high Arctic to southern South America, flying over 2,500 miles without stopping. One of the fastest-flying shorebirds, they have been known to reach speeds of up to 60 mph.

Black-bellied Plover
(*Pluvialis squatarola*)

The Black-bellied Plover is larger than the American Golden-Plover and has a white rump; otherwise they are similar. While both nest in the far North, the Black-bellied is generally only seen on the coasts where it winters and the Golden is generally seen only on migration.

OPPOSITE

Dunlin
(*Calidris alpina*)

Once called the Red-backed Sandpiper, the Dunlin, like all moderate to long-billed shorebirds, probes in the mud to find prey via sensory tactile organs at the end of the bill. The bill has special muscles and hinges that allows it to open only at the tip to capture and suck in prey.

Purple Sandpiper
(*Calidris maritima*)

During the winter the Purple Sandpiper lives on the north Atlantic
coast, scrambling for food items on
rocky outcroppings and pilings while
trying to avoid the jagged surf. This
rotund shorebird winters farther
north than any other shorebird and
is named for an indistinct purple
sheen on its black feathers.

ABOVE

Stilt Sandpiper
(*Calidris himantopus*)

Breeding in the Arctic, the male Stilt
Sandpiper scrapes a depression in the
gravel into which the female lays her
four eggs. The eggs hatch in approximately three weeks and the young
leave the nest only one day later.
Both parents watch over the young
for about two weeks.

Upland Sandpiper
(*Bartramia longicauda*)

While most sandpipers nest in
northerly wetland areas, the Upland
Sandpiper prefers grasslands and
prairies of North America. It chooses
areas of at least 40 acres in size but is
declining due to the disappearance
and fragmentation of its habitat. It
may nest in loose colonies with the
birds synchronizing their breeding.

LEFT

Spotted Sandpiper
(*Actitis macularia*)

The Spotted Sandpiper is probably
the most widespread and abundant
sandpiper in North America. Found
on nearly every river, stream, or lake
margin, its habit of bobbing up and
down, partly for display and partly
to assist in depth perception, makes
it, along with its spots, clearly recognizable.

RIGHT

Spotted Sandpiper Eggs
(*Actitis macularia*)

The Spotted Sandpiper is most often
seen running along the shores of
freshwater lakes and streams, quickly
and frequently bobbing its body up
and down. Like virtually all shorebirds, the nest is a simple depression
in the ground in which four cryptically colored eggs are laid.

TOP

Killdeer
(Charadrius vociferus)

The Killdeer, named for its call, illustrates *disruptive coloration* as the black breast bands break up the bird's outline, making it difficult to spot. It is also known for its broken wing ploy in which it pretends to be injured in order to lure predators to itself and away from its nest.

BOTTOM

American Woodcock
(Scolopax minor)

The woodcock is a medium-sized, roundish, and cryptically-colored shorebird that nests in moist forests. Making its living by probing in the ground for worms and grubs, its eyes are positioned far back in the head allowing a clear rear view. In many states this is a hunted bird.

OPPOSITE

Wilson's Snipe
(Gallinago delicata)

A difficult bird to detect, the snipe remains still until closely approached and then bursts from the ground and flies off very quickly in an erratic, zig-zag pattern. The phrase *snipe hunt*, in which a gullible person is sent off on a fool's errand, may have originated with this bird.

TOP

Whimbrel

(Numenius phaeopus)

The Whimbrel is one of eight kinds of curlew, an old lineage of shorebirds characterized by a long, down-curved bill and brown plumage that changes little throughout the year. The genus name *Numenius* refers to the new moon, a reference to the shape of the bill.

BOTTOM

Whimbrel Eggs

(Numenius phaeopus)

Four eggs are a typical brood of shorebirds. Many shorebirds will eat bits of mollusk or crab shells and even lemming bones, to obtain enough calcium to produce the eggs. Since young birds cannot metabolize salt water in their first few weeks of life, there needs to be a fresh water source nearby.

OPPOSITE

Willet

(Catoptrophus semipalmatus)

Nondescript when wading, its white stripes on black wings are obvious in flight. Like many shore and marsh birds, the Willet will stand on one leg and also perhaps tuck its bill under the feathers of its back. These behaviors prevent heat loss which can be considerable in an aquatic environment.

INDEX

Images by Photographer:

Jim Roetzel: *jacket front, jacket back (1), frontispiece,* 6-7, 8(2), 9, 10, 13(2), 14, 15, 16(right), 18, 19(2), 20-21, 22(2), 25(2), 26-27, 28, 29(2), 31, 32, 33(2), 34(2), 36, 38, 39(2), 40(2), 42(2), 43(2), 44, 45, 46(2), 47, 48-49, 52, 54(2), 55, 57, 62(top), 63, 64, 66(left), 70, 71(2), 72, 73, 74(left), 75, 76(top), 77(2), 78(2), 79(2), 80(2), 81, 82, 83(bottom left), 84(2), 85, 86(2), 87, 88, 89, 90(left), 92(2), 93, 94-95, 98(2), 99, 100, 101(2), 102(bottom), 103, 105(3), 106, 107(top), 108(2), 109, 111, 112(2), 113, 115(2), 116(2), 117, 119, 120-121, 122(top), 124, 125, 126(2), 127, 128, 129, 130-131, 132(2), 133, 134, 135(2), 136, 137, 138(2), 139, 140, 141(2), 142-143, 144(2), 145, 146, 148(2), 149, 151, 152, 153(2), 154(top), 156(2), and 157.

Jim Zipp: *jacket back (2),* 2-3, 5, 11, 12, 16(left), 17, 23, 24, 30(2), 35, 37, 40(bottom, right), 41, 50, 51, 53(2), 56, 58, 59, 60(3), 61, 62(bottom), 65, 66(right), 67, 68(2), 69, 74(right), 76(bottom), 80(left, top), 83(2), 90(right), 91, 96(2), 97, 98(top), 102(top), 104, 107(bottom), 110(2), 114, 118(2), 122(bottom), 123, 126(bottom, left), 147(2), 150, 154(bottom), and 155.

Jim Roetzel is an Ohio native who grew up near Cuyahoga Valley National Park, an area that inspired him to become a nature photographer. An avid hiker, he believes, "being outside matters most; the camera is just a way to share my walks with others."

An enthusiastic bird watcher, Jim's respect for each subject is evident in his photography. He believes that the most important skills of a bird photographer are developed through an understanding of each species and its habitat. This knowledge enables him to create photographs that truly reflect a bird's character.

Jim has photographed throughout the United States and Canada. His work appears in numerous publications, including Twin Lights Publishers' *Cuyahoga Valley National Park* and *Birds of North America*. When not in the field, Jim teaches photography at Hudson City Schools. More of his work can be viewed at www.jimroetzel.com.

Jim Zipp lives in Connecticut where his life revolves around birds. When not in the field photographing or watching birds, he's at The Fat Robin Wild Bird and Nature shop, www.fatrobin.com, a birding shop in Connecticut he owns with his wife Carol.

His first published photograph was of a Saw-Whet Owl in Audubon's *Encyclopedia of North American Birds* in 1980. Jim travels throughout North America in search of new images, with Alaska being a favorite place he returns to again and again.

Jim is represented by agencies around the world and also maintains his own image files. His award winning photographs of the natural world have been featured in publications from *National Geographic, Time* and *Audubon* to *Birder's World, Wildbird, Discovery,* and *ABA's Birding* magazine as well as numerous books and field guides. Jim's images can be seen at www.jimzipp.com.

Dr. Roger J. Lederer is a professional ornithologist who has studied birds for over forty years. He taught ornithology at the university level for 35 years, published 30 scientific studies in professional journals, and is the author of several books in the field of ecology and ornithology, including *Amazing Birds, Pacific Coast Bird Finder* and *Bird Finder*. He has traveled through 80 countries, bird watching in each, and has made hundreds of presentations to community and professional groups, nationally and internationally. Dr. Lederer has written for or consulted with the BBC, *National Geographic*, Weather Notebook, Organic Gardening, National Public Radio, National Canadian Television, *Vanity Fair Magazine, The Guinness Book of World Records*, The Weakest Link, *Real Simple Magazine*, the *Detroit Free Press*, Voice of America, and the Columbia News Service. Although his specific expertise is ornithology, his real focus is environmental education. It is through birds that people can appreciate the beauty and importance of the natural environment and make the important decisions required to protect our natural heritage.